This book is for the beginner karateka who has taken that first step on the journey to "seek perfection of character" and also for the numerous (far too numerous to list all) wonderful martial artists I've had the pleasure of training with all over the world and for my "spiritual" sparring partner, Dr. Barbara Ann Teer

Kim Mu Wong	(Master)	Spain
Lamarr Thornton	(Kushinda)	New York
Kenny Hines	(Sensei)	New York
Richard Dozier	(Sensei)	New York
Darlene DeFour	(Shihan)	New York
Godofredo Echeverria		El Salvador
Ayo Binitie		Ghana
Master Joe		Nigeria
Abdulrahman Atta		Nigeria
Lachezar Nenov	(Sensei)	Bulgaria
Alexander Panov		Bulgaria
Idris Diaz	(Sensei)	Senegal
David Krzywda		USA
Juan Brooks	"Dragon"	USA
Na' im Najieb		New York
Jerry Odum	(Sensei)	North Carolina
Bonaventure	(Sensei)	North Carolina
Tim Pope	(Sensei)	North Carolina
David Fraser		North Carolina
H.P. Henry	(Sensei)	North Carolina
Bradley Cocker (RIP)	(Sensei)	North Carolina
Solomon Kebede	(Sensei)	Ethiopia

Table of Contents

Introduction

As with any new endeavor, Karate-dō for the beginner may seem rather daunting. This handbook for beginners is the first of a two-part book titled "Training for Life – Karate-dō" contains a basic introduction to Karate-do, proper etiquette, practice, philosophy and terminology.

The time spent in class is usually not sufficient to build proficiency in Karate-dō, so make an effort to practice when away from the dōjō. I have included a number of exercises, which may be practiced individually or with a partner.

The purpose of studying Karate-dō is not merely victory or defeat of an opponent in combat, but the practical application of what you have learned to everyday life. Through the practice of karate-do, you should come in contact with the "spirit" of the martial arts and be a critical judge of yourself. Practice Karate-dō diligently and with all seriousness, and you'll acquire the physical, mental and spiritual strength to overcome many challenges in life.

Karate-dō is more than a sport; it is a martial art for the development of character and physical ability through training so that you may acquire the fortitude to overcome many challenges in life.

Karate-dō, which literally means "empty hand way" is a system of self defense which has ancient roots in many Asian countries. Over the years, Karate-dō has been developed and refined into several styles; Shotokan karate popularized by Gichin Funakoshi is perhaps the best known of the Okinawan fighting styles. Today, over ten million people around the world practice Shotokan karate.

There are generally five areas of Karate-dō practice; **UNDO**, which are supplementary exercises that may include running, calisthenics, stretching, and resistance.

REIGI (etiquette), which include traditions from Okinawa, Japan, as well as local traditions, independent thinking, protocols, self discipline and responsible behavior.

KIHON, which are drills focusing on specific techniques or principles. *Kihon* is practiced individually or with one or more partners, with or without equipment.

KATA, which are formal arrangements of techniques executed against imaginary opponents.

KUMITE, which is freeform sparring, involves the execution of techniques against a fellow student or the instructor. As students advance, safeguards are gradually removed until *Kumite* approaches *jissen kumite* or actual fighting.

Kime

Without *Kime*, Karate practice would be no different from dancing; as such, *Kime* is the very essence of Karate. *Kime* means to strike a target with an explosive attack using maximum power in the shortest possible time as if you were engaged in actual combat. *Kime* is not only applied in striking, but in punching, kicking, and blocking as well. A Karate tournament should be no exception, although tournament rules generally forbid the use of "excessive force"

A Karate technique lacking *kime* can never be regarded as true karate, no matter how much the resemblance to karate; however, due to the danger of accidental injury from a powerful attack, one must practice *Kime* together with *Sun dome*. *Sun dome* means to freeze a technique just before contact with the target (one *Sun* is about three centimeters). But not carrying a technique through to *kime* is not true karate, so to reconcile *Kime* with *Sun dome* you should set the target slightly in front of the opponent's vital point, which can then be struck in a controlled way with maximum power, but without making contact.

Kiai

Kiai (気合, 気合い) is a Japanese term that is a compound of *ki* (気) meaning mind, will, turn of mind or spirit and *ai* (合, 合い) being the contraction of the verb *awasu* (合わす), signifying "to unite"; literally "concentrated spirit".

In Karate-dō, *kiai* refers to the shout emitted by the karateka while performing kata or at the moment of executing a technique. The proper use of *kiai* involves concentrating on the use of one's *ki* energy more than it does shouting. In *bujutsu* (Japanese arts of war), it is usually linked to the inner amassing of energy released in a single explosive focus of will. The importance of *kiai* in Karate-dō is in the precise coordination of breathing with the execution of techniques, which may be more accurately referred to as *kokyu* or "breath-power". *Kokyu* and *kiai* are sometimes used interchangeably. A relaxed and powerful exhalation can add power to movement. A sound is just an audible indication of good *kiai* (aligned body structure, focused intent, and good breathing). It's not the sound that is important. The *kiai* is emitted from the *Hara* or *Tanden*, and involves the abdominal muscles and diaphragm; it should not be sounded in the throat.

Hara

The word *Hara* commonly refers to an area a few centimeters (three fingers) below the navel; considered the place where the vital energy is generated and stored. According to Japanese belief, it is here that profound vital forces reside, which is why *ki* is found in the *Hara*, and through the *Hara*, one is able to communicate with the universal energy. In Karate-dō, 'deep' breathing must take place from the *Hara*, because all physical and psychic forces emanate from there. Your techniques will have more power, and your life will be more harmonious when you are able tap into *ki* energy at will by concentrating on and breathing from the *Hara*. The art of concentrating all mental and physical forces on the *Hara* is called *Haragei*.

Dōjō rules and etiquette

Following are the basic rules and etiquette to observe in the dōjō:

1. Bow as you enter or leave the dōjō (this is an expression of courtesy and respect).

2. Bow to the *Sensei* (teacher) as he enters the dōjō. The teacher is addressed as *Sensei* during class. Junior instructors or assistants to the instructor are addressed as *Sempai* (Senior).

3. Follow the formal opening and closing ceremony described below.

4. Class generally begins with the command "*Narande*" (line up). Students line up in front of and facing the *Sensei*, higher ranking students to his/her right. Position in line is determined by rank as well as seniority, i.e. a person who has the rank of *shodan* (first degree black belt) for two years has seniority over a

recent *shodan*.

5.   Talking among students is generally discouraged during class. If you understand an instruction or command, respond with "*Hai*" (yes, ok). If there is something you do not understand or have a question, raise your hand.

6.   During class, when not performing a technique, you should stand only in *heisoku-dachi* (informal attention stance) feet together, arms relaxed, the hands lightly touching the thighs and eyes focused straight ahead, or *Hachiji-dachi* (ready stance); feet shoulder width apart, hands in fists in front of hips and eyes focused straight ahead until *sensei* issues the command to relax. Sloppy posture such as lounging and leaning against walls and actions such as yawning, scratching, or looking around are generally discouraged.

7.   It is considered disrespectful to leave the dōjō during class without first requesting permission from the *Sensei*.

8.   All students are expected to wear a clean plain   white *gi* (traditional karate

uniform); colored or patterned *gi* is not allowed. T-shirts or other garments must not be worn under the *gi* except for girls

9. When adjusting the *gi* or *obi* (belt) the student should turn away from the *sensei* and face the rear of the dōjō.

10. Students must not wear street shoes onto the training area; training is typically done bare feet.

11. Students are encouraged to follow the basic rules of hygiene. Keep fingernails and toenails short. Wash your *gi* regularly (if you train more than twice a week, it is highly recommended to have two *gi*). By tradition, the *obi* should not be washed

12. Students must not wear jewelry or other ornamentation during class. Headbands are generally not allowed except when used by girls to restrain their hair, in which case, they should be white only. Protective pads may not be worn except to protect an injury.

13. Always be on time for class. It is recommended that a student arrive fifteen (15)　minutes before the start of

class; this time should be spent warming up for class. If a student arrives after class has begun, s/he must assume *seiza* (kneeling) position at the rear of the training area until the sensei gives permission to join the class.

Formal opening and closing ceremony

On the command, "*Narande*" (line up), students form a line, highest in rank to the left, lowest in rank to the right. Sensei faces the front of the dōjō, his back to the class. The highest ranking student gives the command, "*seiza*' (formal sitting position) and all kneel and sit back on their heels with backs straight, knees apart approximately the distance of two fists touching those of the students on either side, hands with fingers closed resting on their thighs and eyes straight ahead. With the command "*mokusō*" (to enter a state of medication and clear your mind), all close their eyes for a few moments and try to empty their mind of the day's activities and prepare it for learning. When the word "*mokusō yame*" (stop) is spoken all open their eyes. On the next Command "*shōmen ni rei*" (to the front bow) all bow in unison. Sensei will turn and face the class. Then the senior student will say "*Sensei ni rei*", at which time Sensei and students bow to each other, stand up, and class begins.

At the end of class "*Narande*" (line up), "*seiza*", "*mokusō*" and "*yame*" are commanded as in the beginning. The senior student recites the Dōjō Kun (Karate-dō guiding principles) and all students repeat each line after her/him.

Dōjō Kun
Seek perfection of character
Be faithful
Endeavor
Respect others
Refrain from violent behavior

The senior student says, "*shōmen ni rei*" and "*Sensei ni rei*" as in the beginning. All students then say, "*dōmo arigato gozaimasu*" (thank you) at which time the Sensei will then rise and leave the practice area. At this point, class is officially over and students stand and leave the training area in order of rank.

訓

一、人格完成に努むること
一、誠の道を守ること
一、努力の精神を養うこと
一、礼儀を重んずること
一、血気の勇を戒むること

Basic Techniques (*waza*)

Stances (*dachi*)

Karate-dō is comprised of several stances including special ones that are rarely used except in certain advanced *kata*. The basic stances and perhaps the most frequently used are, *Zenkutsu dachi, Han Zenkutsu dachi, Hachiji dachi, Kiba dachi, Heisoku dachi, and Fudo dachi (Yoi)*. Like the foundation of a building, strong stances provide good balance and a solid base from which to execute powerful karate techniques.

The most vulnerable point in *kata* and *kumite* is during the transition from one stance to another, because the center of gravity is momentarily shifted; keep this in mind as you practice the stances

Zenkutsu dachi (Forward stance)

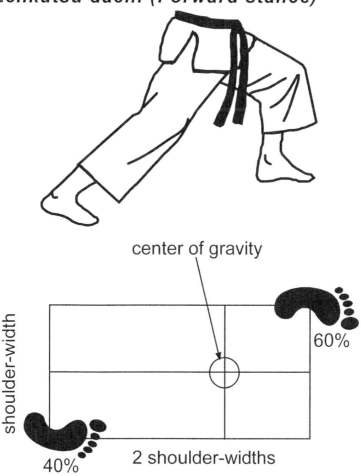

In *zenkutsu dachi*, the forward leg is bent at the knee with 60 percent of the body weight resting on it and 40 percent on the back leg. The knee of the back leg is locked and extended approximately two shoulder-widths behind the lead foot. Keep your upper body straight and your rear foot turned slightly outwards.

Han Zenkutsu dachi (Fighting stance)

Sometimes referred to as the "Short forward stance," *han zenkutsu dachi* actually translates as "half forward stance"

Although it is not as strong defensively in the forward axis thanks to its shorter baseline and higher centre of gravity, it nonetheless compensates by offering greater mobility, and easier hip movement, with a greater range of rotation. *Han zenkutsu dachi* is often called "fighting stance" because it is well suited to *kumite* and resembles the stance taken by boxers

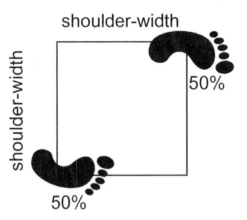

In *han zenkutsu dachi*, your feet are shoulder-width apart and shoulder-width long. Both legs should be slightly bent, allowing the knees to rest naturally. Your weight is evenly distributed between front and back

legs, enabling you to switch your weight onto either leg with ease.

Hachiji dachi

In *hachiji dachi*, the feet are shoulder-width apart with the toes pointing forward. Your body should be upright and facing forward. *Hachiji dachi* is also a *yoi* (ready) position

STEPPING INTO ZENKUTSU DACHI FROM HACHIJI DACHI

To step forward *into zenkutsu dachi* from *hachiji dachi*

Step forward approximately two shoulder-widths with your left leg as your left foot makes a small arc from inside outwards and comes to rest at an angle of 45 degrees (your rear foot should also be at a 45 degree angle, this is *hanmi dachi*). As you step forward, let your sole glide close to the floor, keeping your back upright and eyes looking straight ahead (and not at your feet). Quickly straighten the left foot to point forwards and the back foot slightly outwards, tense the entire body briefly, especially the abdominal muscles. *Hanmi dachi* is a split-second transitional position that allows you to engage the hip in *zenkutsu dachi.*

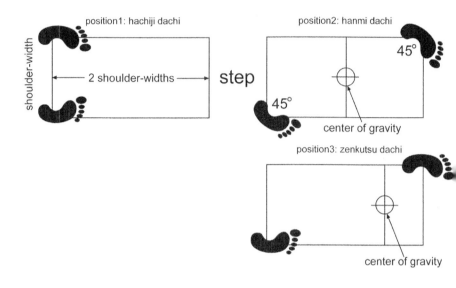

To step backwards into *zenkutsu dachi* from *hachiji dachi*

From *hachiji dachi*, step back with your right leg as your foot makes a small arc from the inside to the outside and comes to rest at an angle of 45 degrees (your lead foot should also be at a 45 degree angle). Most of your body weight should be resting on the front leg. As you straighten up your right foot, push back on the leg, bend the knee of the supporting leg and thrust the left hip forward. Lock the back leg as you tense your entire body briefly

By combining the backward and forward movements of the same leg, you are able to accomplish one giant step. Bring your right foot from the back to the front passing close by the left leg, which should remain bent (try not to bounce up and down) The supply of tension in your supporting leg (in this case, the left) enables you to effectively catapult your body forward. In order to accomplish this, snap your bent supporting leg abruptly forward the moment your right leg passes the supporting leg and push your left hip forward; you should now be in *zenkutsu dachi.* As you place your right foot down, briefly tense your entire body.

As you practice this forward catapulting of your body, keep in mind that the power comes from the supply of tension in your bent supporting leg, which catapults you forcefully forward. Equally pay attention to your rear leg, which must be *thrust out sharply and forcefully.* Increase the tempo gradually while still maintaining good form and always utilizing completely the force of the tension in the bent leg. Your karate movements should be as explosive as a tiger's. Animals crouch when getting ready to spring and in so doing gather the maximum supply of tension; your movement should be no different.

The same principle of catapulting with the aid of a bent supporting leg is equally valid when transitioning into the sideways movements of *kiba dachi*.

Kiba dachi (Straddle leg, or horse stance)

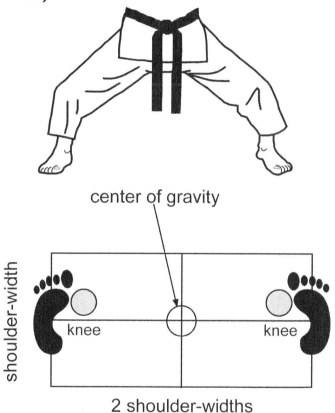

center of gravity

shoulder-width

knee

knee

2 shoulder-widths

In *kiba dachi*, you are in a somewhat seated position (hence the analogy to horse riding) with the feet parallel and roughly two shoulder-widths apart and the toes pointing forwards (Toes pointing outwards is *shiko dachi*, a variation of *kiba dachi*) Since nearly all karate techniques require powerful hip rotations, sitting in *kiba dachi* is considered an excellent way to build strength in the pelvis and thighs.

Fudo dachi, Yoi (Ready stance)

The *yoi* position is a preparatory position that gives a clear starting point for the execution of techniques. In the common version of *yoi*, the arms are slightly moved forward, with fists closed. The fists point slightly to the centre line and are roughly half a shoulder-width apart. The elbows should be bent very slightly.

Punching/Striking Techniques (*Zuki/Uchi Waza*)

All Karate techniques if executed without sufficient control can be potentially lethal, so use extreme caution when practicing punching and striking techniques in *jiyū ippon* or *jiyū kumite*, especially by beginners.

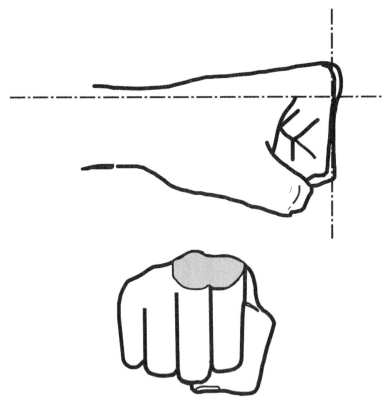

In order to punch correctly in karate, the fingers must be tightly clenched to make a fist and only the knuckles of the middle and index fingers make

contact with the target. For maximum effectiveness
and to minimize the incidence of injury, the fist must
extend straight from the wrist so it doesn't bend at the
point of impact.

Oi zuki (Lunge punch)

In executing *oi zuki*, the punching arm is on the same
side of the body as the leg in front. If you have read
this book this far, then you should have learnt how to
step forward in *zenkutsu dachi*, now combine this
movement with *oi zuki*.   The striking fist and

leading foot should stop at the same time, that is, your fist strikes the target at the same time your lead foot touches down. (Beginners tend to fully step into *zenkutsu dachi* before punching in which case, the power of the momentum generated by the body as it is propelled forwards is completely dissipated)

At the point of impact, your entire body should be tensed momentarily, especially the abdominal muscles as you exhale forcefully through clenched lips

The power of *oi zuki* derives from the momentum of the body as it catapults forward. Practice several times stepping into *zenkutsu dachi* while executing *oi zuki*, and imagine your punching arm is being propelled forward by your body; do not hunch your shoulders. Aim your punch at the face or solar plexus.

Gyaku zuki (Reverse punch)

Gyaku (reverse) as the name implies, is a reverse punch in which the punching arm and front leg, as opposed to *oi zuki*, are reversed. If your right leg is in front, then the punch is made with the left arm and vice versa. The *gyaku zuki* is an extremely powerful punch because it relies on a sharp turning of the hip. *Gyaku zuki* is predominantly used in *jiyū ippon* and *jiyū kumite* for counterattacking because it is not as fast or as direct as *oi zuki*

Gyaku zuki is technically more difficult than *oi zuki* because your fist does not strike at the same time your leading foot touches down; in fact, your punch doesn't even start till after your lead foot has touched down. To execute a *gyaku zuki* while stepping into *zenkutsu dachi*, you first step into *hanmi* (your body is turned at an angle of 45 degrees), which is typically a defensive position, before punching and straightening the body into *zenkutsu dachi*.

Kizami zuki (Jab or Short punch)

Kizami zuki is a jab off the same side as the advancing foot similar to *oi zuki*. *Kizami zuki* is extremely effective as a feint to setup your opponent for a decisive attack, as well as to gauge *mai* (distance). *Kizami zuki* is especially useful when used in combination with *gyaku zuki*.

Take a *han zenkutsu dachi* (the upper body in *hanmi*) facing your opponent with your right foot forward. Your right arm should be bent at the elbow at an angle of 45 degrees with the elbow approximately one fist away from the body and the fist in line with the shoulder. Advance by pulling in your left leg and just before it touches the right leg (the left leg never

29

actually touches the right leg), step forward with the right leg as you snap your right fist towards your target and rotate the forearm and fist at the same time. The strike should begin from your elbow and not your shoulder; as this would be a clear signal to your opponent of an impending attack.

Empi uchi (age empi), up

Empi uchi, elbow strike comes in four variations and each one targets a separate part of the body; *age empi* primarily targets the chin and solar plexus. To practice *age empi*, assume the *kiba dachi* stance with both fists at your side and swing the elbow of the striking arm sharply upwards with the finger side of your fist towards your ear. Because your target is centered relative to your striking elbow, your body must be slightly turned inwards towards the target

Empi uchi (shita empi), down

This variation of the elbow strike primarily targets the back of the neck; as such, it is often used following the execution of a technique such as *hiza geri* (knee kick) to the groin or mid section. *Shita empi* is also effective for striking the insides of an opponent's elbows to release a lapel   grab.

Here is how to practice all four variations of *empi uchi*. Start very slow and focus on correct breathing and form, and then gradually increase the tempo till you reach a point where you can execute all the strikes, both left and right elbow, in rapid succession without pause; *kiai* on the last strike

Assume the *kiba dachi* with both fists at your side, starting first with the right elbow
1. *Age empi* (up) With the hand of the striking elbow in a fist, strike to the middle of the chin
2. *Ushiro empi* (behind) With the hand of the striking elbow open this time, imagine an attacker is attempting to grab you from behind, strike to the mid section
3. *Yoko empi* (to the side, front) Extend your left hand with the palm open, imagine the side of the head (temple, or jaw line), strike your open palm with your elbow (do not pull your palm towards the elbow). The hand of your striking elbow is in a fist
4. *Yoko empi* (to the side, behind) Imagine the attacker attempting to grab you from behind in step 2 succeeded, strike to the attackers head behind you as you   twist your body slightly to

the right (the hand of the striking elbow is once again open)

5. *Shita empi* (down) finally, strike the back of the neck with a *kiai*. Imagine you are pulling down a cord suspended from the ceiling, so the elbow goes up with the hand open and the elbow comes down with the hand in a fist

Now repeat steps 1 through 5 with the left elbow

Often when practicing karate techniques, visualization can be helpful because it allows us to execute our techniques more realistically, with *kime*; this is especially true while practicing *kata*. Practicing the *empi* drill above, try to imagine being assailed by a pair of attackers

Kicking Techniques (*Geri Waza*)

Mae geri (Front kick)

mae geri (front kick) is perhaps by far the most familiar of all the karate kicking techniques. *Mae geri* is a direct frontal kick using the ball of the foot as the striking surface. *Mae geri* comes in two variations; *mae geri keage*, and *mae geri kekomi*

Mae geri keage

Mae geri keage is a snap kick with the knees providing the snapping action. The ball of the kicking foot is thrust upwards ("age" means lift), much like an uppercut punch. The toes must be tightly curled back in order to strike with the ball of the foot. To practice *mae geri keage*, assume the *hachiji dachi* and lift the knee of your right leg as high as possible towards your chest. Keep the raised foot parallel to the floor and toes tightly curled back. Now, quickly snap the raised knee out and back in a single uninterrupted motion; the supporting leg should remain stationary.

Because *mae geri* is a direct frontal kick, be sure that both the foot of the supporting and kicking legs are pointing forward at your target.

Mae geri kekomi

Mae geri kekomi is a forward thrust kick deriving its power from the hip. Just as in the *keage* variant, the ball of the foot is the striking surface, so the toes must be tightly curled back. Both variations of *mae geri* are very effective in *jiyu ippon* and *jiyu kumite*. *Mae geri keage* can be particularly useful as a feint to create an opening, or when the distance between you and your opponent makes it difficult to employ a punching technique. On the other   hand, *mae geri kekomi* is useful for covering distance or stopping your opponent dead in her/his tracks as s/he attempts to launch an attack (this requires very good timing)

Mae tobi geri (Jumping front kick)

Mae tobi geri is basically two mae geri; the first being a feint and the second executed while you are elevated. Although it might appear difficult at first, this is not a particularly difficult kick to learn. Start by facing your opponent with your right foot forward. Pull up the rear leg as if to execute a mai geri. Although this is the feint, it must be done convincingly enough to throw your opponent off balance setting her/him up for the next kick. Before fully extending the left leg, jump up and kick with the right leg.

If possible, practice this attack with a tall sandbag. Spring up from a low position with at most a run of one step. Also try to jump up from a very deep position with the aid of the tension in your legs without a running start. (If the leg with which you are kicking is your right leg, then your right leg is in front.)

KNEE EXERCISE

Place a bench or a chair with a low back in front of you and stand with your back against a wall. Pull your right knee to your chest as tightly as possible and hold it with both hands; do not tilt away at the hip, stay upright. Count to 12. Now release the knee and slowly extend your leg over the bench or chair in front of you; keep the leg extended for at least 3 seconds and carefully pull back to your chest without touching the bench or scraping the back of the chair. Put the leg down and do the same with the left leg; do three sets for each leg.

TARGET PRACTICE

Have a fellow student stand and extend her/his left hand at about chest level height and palms facing down. Take a *zenkutsu dachi* stance facing her/him. Starting with your right leg, kick the extended hand with *mae geri* 10 times. Do the same with the left leg kicking to your partner's right hand. Next, your partner lowers her/his extended hand to stomach level with palms facing out. Assume a *zenkutsu dachi* stance facing her/him. Starting with the right leg, kick your partner's palm with *mae*

36

geri using the ball of the foot (not the toes!)

Your partner could introduce a variation to the practice by randomly switching hands thereby forcing you to adjust quickly and switch legs accordingly.

You must exercise considerable caution as you kick your partner's palm to prevent injury to the wrist.

Yoko geri (Side kick)

Yoko geri (side kick) is another of the popular kicks in Karate-dō. *Yoko geri* is a side kick that uses the outer edge (blade) of the foot as the striking surface. In executing *yoko geri*, your big toe should point up while the rest of your toes point down and your striking foot should point as much downwards as possible. Just like *mae geri*, *yoko geri* comes in two variations; *yoko geri keage*, and *yoko geri kekomi*

Yoko geri keage

As you've probably guessed, *yoko geri keage* is a snap side kick much like the *mae geri keage* with the knees providing the snapping action. To execute *yoko geri keage*, lift your knee up and snap the leg out to the side and pull back quickly before placing the foot down.

Yoko geri kekomi

Yoko geri kekomi is a powerful kick that derives its power from the hip thrust forcefully at the target. In order to engage the hip and add power to *yoko geri kekomi*, it is important to pivot the supporting foot 45 – 90 degrees so that the heel is almost pointing at the target. Do not lean your upper body away from the target so you don't lose your balance. The arm on the same side as the kicking   leg is extended while the other arm stays close to the solar plexus so you are prepared to follow through the *yoko geri* with a striking technique or simply to block a counterattack. Practice *yoko geri* from the *kiba dachi* stance

STRETCHING EXERCISE FOR *YOKO GERI*

Assume a *kiba dachi* in front of your partner with your right side facing her/him; your partner should be in *hachiji dachi*. The distance between you and your partner should be such that when you step in with the left leg and extend the right leg in *yoko geri* your foot barely touches your partner's chest. Without raising your body, step towards your partner by crossing the left leg in front of the right, lift your knee as high as possible, if necessary, with the aid of your hand. Slowly extend your leg in *yoko geri kekomi* barely touching your partner's chest as s/he takes your foot in both hands and pushes it higher; tap your leg to signal your partner to stop pushing the moment you begin to feel pain or discomfort. Pull your upper body up towards your partner staying as upright as possible. Make sure the heel of the supporting leg is pointing towards the extended leg, your left arm close to the solar plexus and right arm extended over the kicking leg. As your partner lets go of your foot, retract it fully before setting it down gently and stepping back into *kiba dachi*. Taking turns with your partner, do this ten times with the right leg then switch to the left

Mawashi geri (Roundhouse kick)

Mawashi geri (roundhouse kick) is another popular kick in Karate-dō. *Mawashi geri* is executed with the ball of the foot or the instep as the striking surface and derives its power from a forceful hip rotation. In order to fully engage the hip and lend power to your *mawashi geri*, the supporting foot must pivot 90 degrees with the heels almost pointing at the target.

Have a fellow student stand in front of you and extend their right hand as if to   shake your hand (this should be no higher than stomach level). Take a *han zenkutsu dachi* stance, left leg in front facing her/him. Now execute *mawashi geri* in two steps; step 1, lift your knee up to the side, step 2, slowly extend the leg from the knee in *mawashi geri* and strike your partner's palm lightly, while at the same time pivoting the supporting foot 45-90 degrees. Retract the foot to step 1 before placing it down gently. Taking turns with your partner, do this ten times off each leg. This exercise is not about how fast or high you can kick, it is intended to build strength, specifically in the muscles that are utilized in *mawashi geri*

STRETCHING EXERCISE FOR *MAWASHI GERI*
Start with you and your partner facing each other. Your partner assumes a *zen kutsu dachi* while you take a *han zenkutsu dachi* with your left leg forward. Slowly extend your right leg in *mawashi geri* aiming directly at your partner's head and bring your foot to rest on her/his shoulder. Your partner holds your foot firmly on her/his shoulder and begins to rise slowly from the *zenkutsu dachi* into an upright standing position. Do not lean your upper body too far back, try to stay upright. Your right arm should be slightly extended while the left arm stays close to the solar plexus. Make sure the foot of the supporting leg is

pointing 45-90 degrees away from the extended leg. As your partner raises her/his body, tap your leg to signal the point where the stretching is becoming too painful; do not stretch beyond the point of pain as this could lead to injury to the hamstrings

Pivoting Exercise

Take a *han zenkutsu dachi* with the right leg forward. Step forward and lift your left knee up as you quickly pivot the foot of your supporting right leg 45-90 degrees (the heel should be pointing forward, that is, your toes pointing backwards) Place the left foot down in front so that your right leg is now behind. Now step forward and lift your right knee as you quickly pivot the supporting left foot. Depending on the size of the space where you are practicing, step as many times back and forth as the space will allow.

EXERCISE TO IMPROVE BALANCE

Take a *han zenkutsu dachi* stance and bring your right knee up with the foot to the side as you grab your ankle with your right hand. Release your ankle and slowly extend the leg in *mawashi geri*, then retract the leg and grab the ankle again without placing the foot down. Extend the right leg in this way

42

ten times before switching to the left leg. Through out this exercise, your knees must maintain the same level; do not drop them and do not let them bounce up and down. When you succeed in doing this exercise without hopping around on your supporting leg or have to hold onto an object to regain your balance, you will have achieved excellent balance!

Hiza geri (Knee kick)

The knee kick is a very powerful close quarter technique mainly used to attack the groin, stomach or head. It can also be done from the side to attack the ribs. Grabbing your opponent and pulling them into your knee kick makes the knee strike even more powerful.

HOW TO PERFORM A KNEE KICK

Usually performed with the rear leg, the kick should start from your heel by using your toes to push off, thus springing forward, forcing your knee at your opponent. The target can be the groin or the solar plexus. Against heavier opponents, pull yourself into the opponent, knee first. Opponents of similar or lesser weight can be pulled into the knee to make the technique more effective.

EXERCISES TO IMPROVE KICKING TECHNIQUE
Following are a number of exercises that will greatly improve kicking technique and require only a few minutes of practice. Do them at home or as warm-up drills prior to a training session.

The legs are very potent weapons with a wide range of motion; however, in order to use them effectively, you must practice frequently.

Here is an exercise you can do everyday. Assume the *hachiji dachi* and lift your right knee so your thigh is parallel to the floor. Execute ten rapid *mae geri keage*, snapping the knee out and back; try and maintain the knee at the same height for all ten kicks. Without putting your leg down, turn sideways (the foot of the supporting leg turned 45-90 degrees away from the kicking leg) and execute ten rapid *mawashi geri* without dropping the knee. Now repeat the same for the left leg. This exercise in addition to increasing the power of your kicks also improves balance.

If kicking technique lacks accuracy, then training for power and speed is pointless; you should be able to strike the "bulls eye" with your kicks 9 times out of ten! Here is an exercise to develop accuracy in kicking techniques. Attach a string to a tennis ball and suspend it from the ceiling to about chest level. Assume a *han zenkutsu dachi* facing the ball. Starting with *mae geri keage*, with your right leg, kick at the ball with full power ten times freezing your kick just before striking the ball (*sun dome*) Next, execute ten *yoko geri keage* and ten *mawashi geri* off the right leg before switching to the left leg. As you progress, you should adjust the height of the ball till you reach head level (for those who are pretty flexible). This exercise in addition to developing accuracy in your kicks also improves control (*sun dome*)

A combination kicking exercise is an excellent training method certain to improve overall kicking technique. Feel free to make up your own combinations. Here is one of my favorite combinations; I recommend you practice it often.

Take a *han zenkutsu dachi* with the left leg forward. With your right leg, execute *mae geri*, and *yoko geri* without putting the leg down in between techniques. Put the right leg down in front so your left leg is behind, now repeat the   combination with your left leg; you should be advancing after each combination. Through out this exercise, try not to drop the knee in between kicks, keep the knee as high as possible.

Here is an exercise to practice with a partner. Have your partner take a *zenkutsu dachi* while holding a kicking pad, if one is available, to her/his midsection. If there is no kicking pad, you may kick your partner's abs using medium power. To absorb the force of your kicks, your partner should shift slightly backwards at the moment of impact. Take a *han zenkutsu dachi* stance left foot forward facing your partner. Execute a *mae geri kekomi* straight to your partners midsection with the intention of pushing her/him back. Place your right foot down in front as your partner steps backwards in *zenkutsu dachi*. Now kick at your partner with the left leg and continue with the right leg and so on till you are restricted by the size of the practice area. The object of this exercise is to develop accuracy, distancing, power and control.

Blocking Techniques (*Uke Waza*)

GEDAN BARAI OR GEDAN UKE (LOW BLOCK)

Gedan barai is executed with the external edge of your lower arm approximately two inches above your wrist by sharply striking the attacking limb downwards; *gedan barai* is typically practiced in *zenkutsu dachi*.

In principle, *gedan barai* can be applied from any position; however, it is best practiced from *zenkutsu dachi* (forward stance). To execute *gedan barai* with the right arm, start from *hachiji dachi* with your arms crossed at the solar plexus; the blocking (right) arm is on top with the fist close to the left ear. As you step forward with your right leg into *zenkutsu dachi*, cut a sharp downward arc with your right arm and at the same time pull back the left arm to your left hip. Your hips should be in *hanmi*. The blocking (right) arm should stop at the same time your right foot is placed down and the fist should be approximately 10 inches above the knee.

SOTO (CHUDAN) UKE (OUTSIDE MIDDLE BLOCK)

Soto uke uses the outer (soto) edge of the lower arm. To execute soto uke with your right arm, start by bringing your right fist up beside your right ear and the left arm extended straight out in front of you; both hands should be in fists. As you pull your left arm to your left hip, snap your right arm across your chest and twist your hip and wrist so that the knuckles are facing forward. The fist of the blocking (right) hand should be close to the opposite (left) shoulder and the

49

elbow should be above the thigh of the right leg.

UCHI (CHUDAN) UKE (MIDDLE BLOCK)

Uchi uke is executed with the inner (*uchi*) edge of the lower arm; *uchi uke* is typically practiced in *zenkutsu dachi*.

To execute *uchi uke*, start with the fist of your right hand close to your left hip, palm open. Using your elbow as a pivotal point, snap your arm upwards towards the opposite (right) shoulder. Your elbow should not swing out past   your body; it should

50

remain in front of your body.

AGE (JODAN) UKE (HIGH BLOCK)

Age uke is primarily used to block (strike) attacks to the face and head. The attacking arm is struck from underneath in an upward motion, either with the fist or the open hand. As you execute *age uke*, turn your wrist so that your knuckles face you and the outside bony edge of your lower arm is in front of your

51

forehead. Turn your body to the side as you stop the strike. Do not allow your elbows to extend beyond the sides of your body. When practicing *age uke* in *zenkutsu dachi*, the elbow of your blocking arm should be in a position directly above the middle of the thigh of your forward leg.

EXERCISE TO IMPROVE BLOCKING TECHNIQUE
This exercise is a slight variation on *jiyu ippon kumite*. Working with a partner the both of you assume *hachiji dachi* and stand close enough so that if your partner extends her/his hand, it will slightly touch your solar plexus. Now your partner punches right-left *jodan* (high), right-left *chudan* (middle), and right-left *gedan* (low), while you block, left-right *age uke*, left-right *chudan uke*, and left-right *gedan uke*. When you have become comfortable with the rhythm, have your partner change the rhythm and sequence of the punches from right-left to left-right.

Training Tips

Blocking and counter attacking

Turning your hip is the decisive factor in being able to block and then counter attack. As you block, your body should be turned away slightly in *hanmi* allowing you turn your hip in a counter attack. You must learn to snap you hip back and forth; this is how you generate power in all karate techniques.

45°

Age (jodan) uke with the right arm and the body in *hanmi*; notice the positioning of the left arm in preparation to counter attack with *gyaku zuki*

BLOCKING AND COUNTER ATTACKING FROM
HACHIJI DACHI TO *ZENKUTSU DACHI*

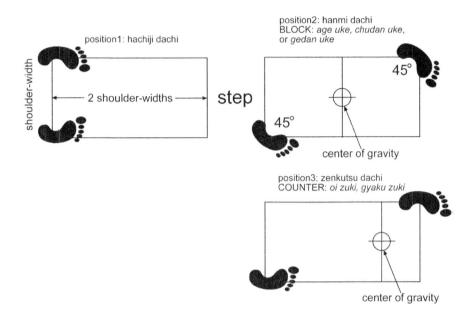

To block and counter from *hachiji dachi* to *zenkutsu dachi*

From *hachiji dachi*, step forward approximately two shoulder-widths with your left foot making a small arc from inside outwards and coming to rest at an angle of 45 degrees (your rear foot should also be at a 45 degree angle, this is *hanmi dachi*). At the same time, execute *age uke*, *chudan uke* or *gedan uke* with your left arm. Now snap your   hip forward into *zenkutsu dachi* as you counter attack with *gyaku zuki*, tense the entire body briefly, especially the abdominal muscles; *kiai* on the *gyaku zuki*. Remember that *Hanmi dachi* is a split-second transitional position that allows you to powerfully engage the hip in a counter attack.

Stepping back

From *zenkutsu dachi*, step back with your left leg as your foot makes a small arc from the inside to the outside and coming to rest at an angle of 45 degrees (your lead foot should also be at a 45 degree angle). Most of your body weight should be resting on the front leg. At the same time, execute *age uke*, *chudan uke* or *gedan uke* with your right arm. Now snap your hip forward into *zenkutsu dachi* as you counter attack with *gyaku zuki*; lock the back leg as you tense your entire body briefly

By combining the backward and forward movements of the same leg, you are able to accomplish one giant step. Bring your right foot from the back to the front passing close by the left leg, which should remain bent (try not to bounce up and down) The supply of tension in your supporting leg (in this case, the left) enables you to effectively catapult your body forward. In order to accomplish   this, snap your bent supporting leg abruptly forward the moment your right leg passes the supporting leg and push your left hip forward; you should now be in *zenkutsu dachi*. As you place your right foot down, briefly tense your entire body.

Developing elasticity in the knees

The knees play an important role in karate techniques. As you advance in karate, you will need to develop elasticity in your knees in order for your techniques to be effective. The importance of elasticity in the knees is most evident when stepping from one stance into another. In the previous example when we stepped from *hachiji dachi* to *zenkutsu dachi*, in the transitional *hanmi dachi*, the knees are relaxed and slightly bent, and not tensed prematurely before switching to *zenkutsu dachi*. This requires considerable elasticity in the knees, which is the key to being able to engage the hip when counter attacking. When you execute *gyaku zuki*, the power comes from the rear leg and hip as they are pushed forward by straightening the bent knee of the rear leg.

We already know how to step from *hachiji dachi* into *zenkutsu dachi*; this is also a good exercise for developing elasticity in the knees. To start, place your thumbs in your obi (belt) and with the left foot making a small arc from inside, step out from *hachiji dachi* into *hanmi dachi* and quickly twist your hip into *zenkutsu dachi* by straightening up the knee of the back (right) leg. Step forward five times and then back. Don't lean forward or take a "deep" *zenkutsu dachi* so as not to put undue pressure on the knees.

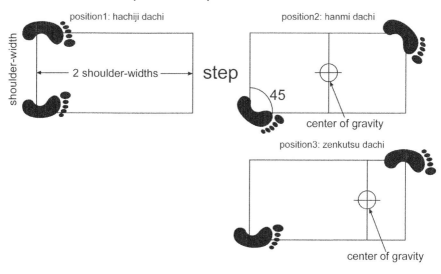

Developing speed and force in techniques

Speed and force are two very important elements in karate techniques. Scientifically, a force is described as a push or a pull on an object that will cause a stationary object to move or a moving object to change direction, slow down, or speed up. While speed is described as a   measure of how fast something is moving. Speed is measured by dividing the distance traveled by the time taken to travel that distance.

As a karateka, having speed is a good thing, but not good enough when there is no force. So, not only do you want to strike with speed, you also want your strikes to have sufficient force to "cause a stationary object to move or a moving object to change direction"

All karate techniques combine "tensing" and "relaxing" of the muscles. Speed is only possible when the muscles are relaxed. Tension is only introduced at the moment of impact. This is why correct breathing is fundamental for mastery of karate-do techniques.

Physical movement induces the contraction of muscle fibers to varying degrees. For instance, bending your arms at the elbows will induce contraction of the bicep muscle, this contraction or shortening of the muscle fibers is known as isotonic contractions. In contrast, Isometric contraction occurs when there is tension on a muscle but no movement is made that induces a shortening of the muscle fibers. In isometric contractions, your muscles contract but your joints don't move and muscle fibers maintain a constant length. For example, leaning forward and pressing your palms against an immovable wall will induce tension in your muscle but no movement is made causing the length of the muscle to remain the same.

The principle of Isometric contractions has been found to be very effective in developing total strength of a particular muscle or group of muscles. A number of bodybuilders incorporate various forms of isometric exercises in their training routines; with a little bit of creativity, you too can make up your own isometric exercises.

Although we can all think of a great many isometric exercises, the focus should be on those forms of exercises that complement karate-do practice. In karate-do practice, the body is generally free of tension except at the moment of impact, when the entire body is tensed momentarily. Therefore, consider isometric exercises that follow this pattern of "relaxing" and "tensing" of the muscles, especially the abdominals.

The most important   consideration for any

isometric exercise is correct breathing. Always assume a straight position such as standing or sitting straight up with shoulders back so that the spine is properly aligned. To derive the most benefit from your isometric exercise, use a steady rhythmic breathing from the *hara* to ensure proper "relaxing" and "tensing" of the muscles as well as sufficient oxygen circulation.

Training for Life

The motto of the Karate-dō governing body, the Japan Karate Association (JKA) reads;

"The primary aim in the art of karate is neither victory nor defeat; the true karate contestant strives for the perfection of his/her character."

The above statement clearly demonstrates that the purpose of Karate-dō training goes beyond the mastery of technique or victory over an opponent. Rather, the concept of triumph over "oneself" suggests that the practitioner's real objective is to seek the perfection within his/her character.

Is it possible to attain "the perfection of character" in a lifetime? The founding fathers of the JKA by using the word strive, fully recognized that seeking "perfection of character" is a work in progress that requires constant effort, tremendous discipline and life-long commitment.

Karate-dō training provides the foundation to seek the "perfection of character" Typically, training begins with learning basic stances, which at first seem awkward and make little or no sense, then followed by *kihon* (drills focusing on specific techniques or principles), which are extremely challenging. Mastery of *kihon* requires concentration, constant practice, the courage to be self-critical and the ability to approach complicated and difficult techniques with a desire for deep understanding. This form of training demands and develops certain qualities –concentration, focus, perseverance, and self-discipline – which invariably help the practitioner to overcome obstacles in life.

Karate-dō training challenges the practitioner in ways that reflect the challenges faced in everyday life. It therefore represents a sort of "school of life." This quickly becomes apparent to the beginner Karate-dō practitioners who often begin with a lot of enthusiasm and motivation after having watched a number of martial arts movies. However, for some, enthusiasm is quickly dampened at the realization that mastery of techniques will require many years of rigorous and committed training. Most beginners hoping to impress friends with their newly acquired skills after only a few weeks of training are soon disappointed, and those hoping to perhaps use their newly acquired skills to intimidate others quickly lose interest. A significant number of beginners, those seeking instant gratification, will quit   training after only a few weeks or maybe months. All too often a "quick fix" characterizes their overall attitude to life. Their lack of discipline and perseverance will impact whatever endeavor in life they may engage in.

Karate-dō training poses no danger to the practitioner any more than say, a game of basketball. Although real mastery of Karate-dō requires diligent and committed training, it is well worth the investment in time and effort. Karate-dō (including ju jutsu and other martial arts) training when undertaken as a lifelong commitment confers tremendous benefits to the practitioner.

Appendices

Glossary of Japanese words used frequently in Karate

PRONUNCIATION

Vowels are pronounced as follows:

a – ah

e – eh

i – ee

o   oh

u – ooh

r – l

In general, each syllable in a word is pronounced with the same emphasis. The 'R' sound is usually rolled and sounds very close to an 'L'. Trailing 'U's' are often silent as in *Kudsurogu* and *Desu*, which are pronounced *Kudsurog* and *Des*.

NUMBERS
Ichi	One
Ni	Two
San	Three

Shi	Four
Go	Five
Roku	Six
Shichi	Seven
Hachi	Eight.
Ku	Nine
Ju	Ten

A

Age	Rising
Age tsuki	Rising punch
Age uke	Rising block
Ana ta no catch	(You are) Winner
Arigato	Thank you
Ashi barai	Foot sweep
Ashi kubi	Ankle
Ashi waza	Foot techniques
Atemi	Strike
Atemi waza	Striking techniques

B

Budo	Martial arts Way
Bunkai	Application (break down) of kata techniques
Bushi	Warrior class of Japan

Bushido	Way of the warrior
Bujutsu	Martial arts techniques
C	
Choku tsuki	Straight punch
Chudan	Midsection of the body
Chudan uke	Middle block
D	
Dachi	Stance
Dan	Black belt rank
De ashi barai	Front foot sweep
Denzook	No count
Do	The way
Dōjō	Martial arts training hall, literally "Place of the Way"
E	
Empi	Elbow
Empi uchi	Elbow strike
F	
Fukushin	Judge
Fumikomi geri	Stomping kick
G	
Ganmen	Face
Ganmen	Knife hand attack to the face

shuto

Gatame	Hold, arm bar
Geashi	Reversal
Gedan	Lower part of the trunk
Gedan barai	Low block
Gedan juji uke	Lower X block
Gedan shuto uke	Lower knife hand block.
Geri	Kick.
Gi	Abbreviation for traditional Karate Uniform. The correct term would be *Karategi*
Go	Five
Gyaku	Reverse, reversal
Gyaku tsuki	Reverse punch
H	
Hachi	Eight
Hachiji dachi	Open leg stance
Hai	Yes, ok
Haishu	Back of the hand
Haishu uchi	Back hand strike
Haisoku	Instep
Haisoku geri	Instep kick
Haito	Ridge hand, inner blade of hand

Haito uchi	Ridge hand strike
Hajimae	Begin
Hansoku	Foul
Hantei	Decision
Harai	Sweep
Hidari	Left
Honbu	Headquarters
I	
Ibuki	Controlled breathing
Ichi	One
Ippon	Point (as in scoring)
Ippon Kumite	One step sparring
J	
Jiyu Kumite	Freestyle sparring
Jodan	Head
Jodan Juji uke	High X block
Ju	Ten
Ju Dachi	Free Fighting stance
Juji	Cross
Juji uke	X block
K	
Karate	Literally, "empty hand", or weaponless

Karateka	One who practices karate
Kata	Stylized form, pre arranged techniques
Katame	Grappling
Keri waza	Kicking techniques
Ki	Life force
Kiai	The shout a karateka makes as s/he makes a strike
Kibadachi	Straddle (horse) stance
Kime	Focus.
Kingeri	Groin kick.
Kokutsu dachi	Rear weighted open stance – front heel raised
Koshi	Ball of the foot
Ku	Nine
kobudo	Weapons training
Kudasai	Please (if you please).
Kudsurogu	Relax or rest
Kumiuchi	Grappling
Kumite	Sparring
Kyu	Colored belt rank
L	
M	
Mae	Front
Mae geri	Front kick

Mae geri keage	Front snap kick
Mae geri kekomi	Front thrust kick
Mae tobi geri	Jump front kick
Makiwara	Board used to toughen hands, feet, knees and elbows by striking it
Mawashi geri	Roundhouse kick
Mawahshi tsuki	Roundhouse punch
Mawatte	Turn
Migi	Right (side)
Mikazuki	Crescent
Mikazuki geri	Crescent kick
Mokusu	Contemplation
Morote uke	Augmented block
Musubi Dachi	Attention stance
N	
Namiashi	Sweep avoidance
Neko	Cat
Neko ashi dachi	Cat stance

Ni	Two
Nidan geri	Double jump kick
Nukite	Spear hand
O	
Obi	Belt
Oi tsuki	Lunge punch
Okuri ashi barai	Foot sweep
P	
Q	
R	
Rei	Bow
Roku	Six
Ryu	School of martial arts
Ryukyu	Okinawa
S	
San	Three
Sanchin dachi	Hourglass stance
Satori	Enlightenment
Seiza	Kneeling/Sitting position
Sempai	Senior
Sensei	Teacher
Seridsu	Line up
Shikkaku	Disqualification

Shuto	Knife hand
Shuto uchi	Knife hand strike
Shuto uke	Knife hand block
Soto	Outside (of opponent's stance)
Soto uke	Outside block (from outside to center)
Soto mikazuki geri	Outer crescent kick (from outside to center)
Soto shuto	Outside knife hand block
Suwari	Sit

T

Taisabaki	Body twisting evasion movements
Tatte	Stand up
Te	Hand
Teisho	Palm heel
Teisho tsuki	Palm heel punch
Teisho uchi	Palm heel strike
Teisho uke	Palm heel block
Tenshin Sho	Divine intervention
Tettsui	Hammer fist
Tsuki	Punch using first two knuckles only

U

Uchi	Inner
Ude	Forearm
Ude uke	Forearm block

Uke	Block
Uraken uchi	Back fist strike
Uratsuki	Close punch
Ushiro	Rear
Ushiro geri	Back kick
V	
W	
Wado	Second Largest style of Japanese Karate Worldwide. Directly translated, it means "Way of Peace and Harmony".
Wazari	Half point
X	
Y	
Yama	Mountain
Yamabushi	Mountain warriors
Yamagomori	Craziness in the mountains
Yawara	Control
Yamei	Stop.
Yodansha	One who is a black belt
Yoi	Ready
Yoko	Side
Yoko geri	Sidekick
Yoko haito	Side ridge hand
Yoko	Side thrust kick

kekome

Yoko shuto   Side knife hand

Yoko tobi   Jump sidekick

geri

Z

Zanshin   Awareness of opponent

Zazen   Sitting meditation

Zen   Buddhist sect. Religious meditation.

Zenkutsu   Forward stance – front leg bent, back

dachi   leg straight

About the Author

Sensei Andrew Igbo has over 25 years experience training and teaching martial arts and self defense to diverse populations.

He began Tae kwon do training in September 1980 under Master Kim Mu Wong in Madrid, Spain and obtained a black belt in the fall of 1984. He began Shotokan Karate training in January 1991 under *Kushinda* Lamar Thornton in Harlem, New York and obtained *shodan* (1st degree black belt) in 1993 and present rank, *sandan* (3rd degree black belt) in 1995.

Sensei Andrew Igbo is also training in Kali, Ju Jutsu under Shihan Darlene DeFour and Sensei Kenny Hines, and Kobudo under HP Henry Sensei and Sensei Tim Pope.

Printed in Great Britain
by Amazon